Bones, Bones, Dinosaur Bones
by Byron Barton

A TRUMPET CLUB SPECIAL EDITION

Published by The Trumpet Club, 666 Fifth Avenue, New York, New York 10103.   Copyright © 1990 by Byron Barton.
All rights reserved.   For information address: HarperCollins Publishers, New York, New York.
ISBN: 0-440-84313-8
This edition published by arrangement with HarperCollins Publishers.   Printed in the United States of America.   September 1991.
10 9 8 7 6 5 4 3 2 1
UPC

Bones. Bones. We look for bones.

Tyrannosaurus, Apatosaurus, Stegosaurus, Ankylosaurus, Parasaurolophus, Gallimimus, Thecodontosaurus, Triceratops.

We look for the bones of dinosaurs.

We find them.

We dig them up.

We wrap them

and pack them.

We load them on trucks.

We have the bones of dinosaurs.

We have head bones, foot bones, leg bones,

rib bones, back bones, teeth and claws.

We put the claws on the foot bones

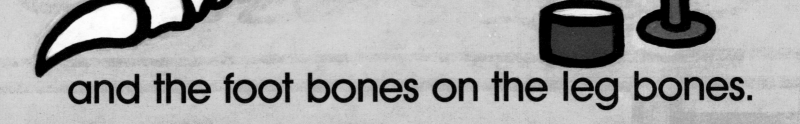

and the foot bones on the leg bones.

We put the teeth in the head bones

and the head bones on the neck bones.

We put the rib bones on the back bones.

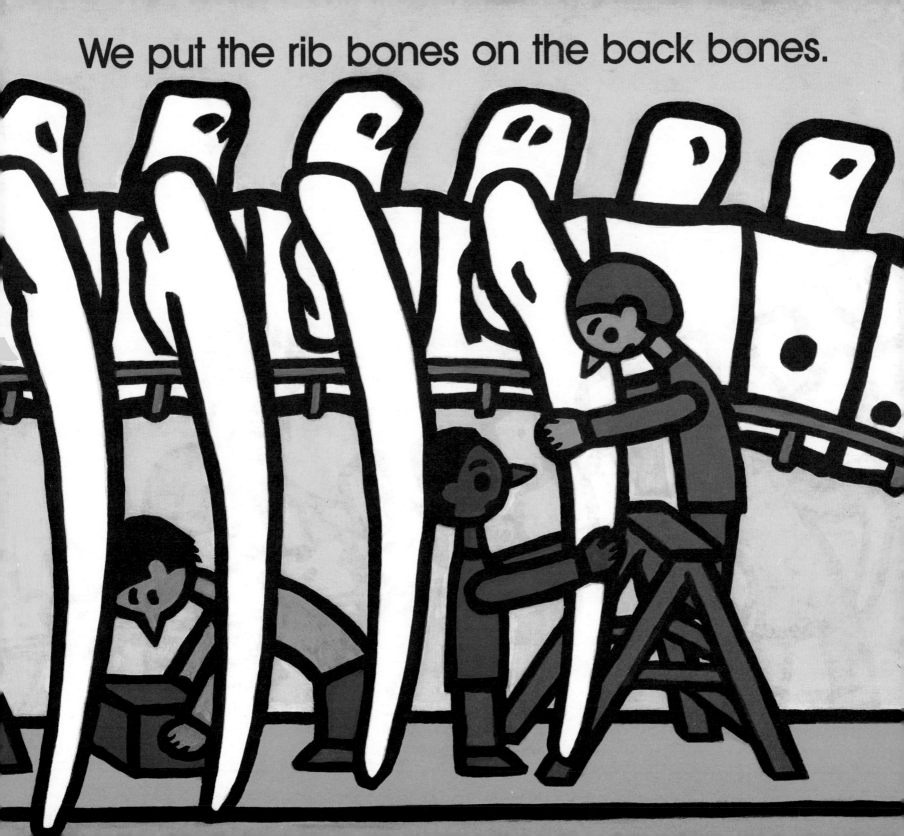

And the tail bones are last.

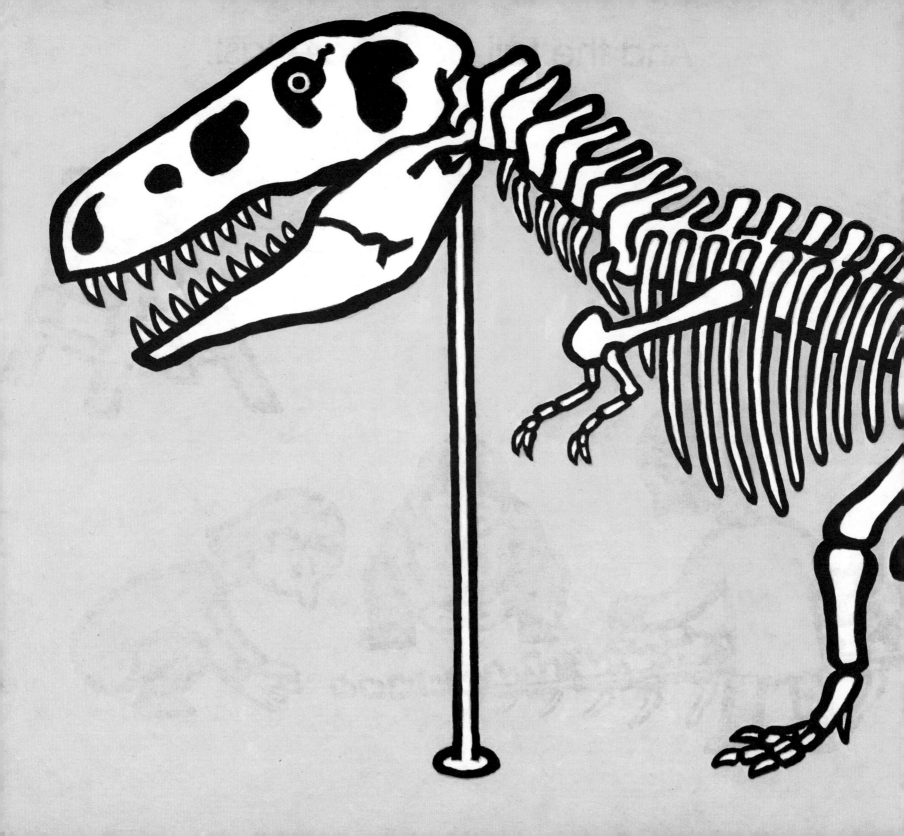

These are the bones of Tyrannosaurus rex.

Bones. Bones. We look for bones.

Tyrannosaurus rex
(ty-ran-oh-SAW-rus rex)

Ankylosaurus
(an-KY-loh-SAW-rus)

Thicodontosaurus
(thee-coh-don-toh-SAW-rus)

Triceratops
(try-SARE-ah-TOPS)

We look for the bones of dinosaurs.